BALLA
from the PUBS *of*
IRELAND
Volume 1
POPULAR SONGS & BALLADS

by James N. Healy

OSSIAN

published in association
with Mercier Press

To all Poteen stood for

Music artwork and Guitar chords by Lochlin Scully
Design by John Loesberg
Cover Photo: © Bord Failte
Printed by Colour Books, Dublin

OSSIAN PUBLICATIONS LTD.
P.O.Box 84, Cork, Ireland
E Mail: ossian@iol.ie

OMB 116
ISBN 1 900428 30 X

Preface

All the songs in this book are meant to be sung, and, to be honest it is mostly in pubs that I have heard them. Not all may meet the approval of the purest folk-song collector, but in their different states and forms they have all come from the people.

Long before people in Ireland began writing ballads in English there were thousands of songs and ballads all over the country in Irish. Following the imposition of the Penal Laws at the end of the seventeenth century English began to gradually replace the native language, and the danger was that much of the old material would be lost: indeed much has been, but Edward Bunting was commissioned at the end of the eighteenth century to gather many of the old harpers together and take down the old tunes from them. Later lyricists used these tunes for songs in English, as well as being awakened to other source material, so that a great deal of what might have faded with memory was preserved for future generations, and gave a rich source of tunes for balladmakers to hang their verses on. These songsters came from several moulds – one, those emanating from the simple rural people who at the beginning had an imperfect use of the new language they had adopted. They recorded events as they happened, and these, whatever the literary shortcomings, are the true ballads.

Many people from the leisured classes used the old tunes in a more literary form, and Tom Moore was one of a number who took full advantage of them – often changing the original character of the air to suit the sometimes saccharine verses he wrote to them. Just the same who could match the best of Moore? It is by a man's best work that he must be judged.

When I first brought out *Ballads from the Pubs* twenty years ago a number of people, many now gone, helped me. I remember them with gratitude. Now the format is different and I have introduced several new numbers, particularly translations from old Irish drinking songs which seemed appropriate to the title, and others, for various reasons, I have replaced. The notes have also been constructed in the interest of being able to present all the tunes fully and with words and guitar chords.

I have made every effort to make and check acknowledgements of authors and composers, and to ensure that copyright material is not printed without permission; the origin of some ballads is so obscure that it is impossible to be certain that one has covered all the ground. If any due acknowledgements have not been made I hope this note will be taken as sufficient atonement.

James N. Healy.

January 1985

Contents

10. Pléaráca na Ruarcach (O'Rourke's Feast)   26

Brian O'Rourke, Prince of Breffni, was hanged, drawn and quartered by the British in 15?1 for what they called treason. He did not understand English, but when told what the charge was answered: 'If that is so, let it be.' He had waged war continually against the forces of Elizabeth.

In contrast to this grim reminder of his end the song is a riotous description of the Christmas festivities at his Castle of Dromahaire. The song which I have translated was written and composed in the eighteenth century.

The drawing is a caricature of an old feast illustration.

III. WANDERING POETS AND BALLADMAKERS

11. The Bard of Armagh   30

The old bards of Ireland had power in their ability to lampoon and defame. But bards, like everyone else grew old, and then the fingers of the harp strings moved more slowly.

12. The Shilling a Night   31

Eoghan Roe Ward travelled the roads of Ireland in the 1940s with a black donkey and a cart describing himself as 'The Bard of Tirconnail' and the 'Last of the Bards'. His real name was Patrick O'Connell. I met him in Ardmore, County Waterford, where he gave me the ballad sheet of 'A Shilling a Night', and wrote on the back of it for me:
> 'Tis tight to pull against the ebb.
> And easy to flow with it. Have you tried?

13. Ól-dán Seán Ó Tuama (John Twomey's Drinking Song).   33

One of the last nests for wandering bards in the old tradition of the Gaelic tongue was centred on the public house of Seán Ó Túama in Croom, County Limerick. His companions in verse eventually drank him out of house and home. He died in 1775, aged sixty-nine and received the tribute of an enormous funeral attended by bards, balladmakers and poets of every degree who had remembered the days when he proudly and lavishly dispensed hospitality to all.

14. An Bunnán Buíde (The Yellow Bittern).   34

Cathal Buíde MacGiolla Gunna (Charles Gunn) was from County Cavan and died around the middle of the eighteenth century.

One day in freezing weather he found a bittern – dead because it was unable to get a drink from the frozen lake. Since Cathal Buíde appreciated a drink himself he felt in sympathy with the bird's fate.

The translation is by Thomas MacDonagh, one of those executed after the 1916 Rising.

15. The Oul' Triangle   37

Brendan Behan was in his way, and with the development of modern times, a bard in his own right. Wayward, but essentially gentle and humane, he would be the first to admit that he himself quite deliberately and impishly added to a public image which did not at all fully express the character of a man who had the sorrows of the downtrodden of the world very much at heart. When bringing out the original form of this book, just after he had died, his widow Beatrice gave me permission to include this ballad which echoes so poignantly over the prison court-yard from an unseen voice as the curtain rose and fell on his play *The Quare Fellow*.

IV. SPORTING OCCASIONS

16. The Bould Tadhy Quill   38

The Bould Tadhy Quill was written by Johnny Pat Gleeson who came from the mountains between Macroom and Millstreet. It has been ringing lustily in the pubs of Cork, in particular, for sixty years.

young, was renowned for his vigorous and quite out-of-tune rendition. It probably came from Dublin and was certainly carried on by the racing fraternity. I am indebted to George Briscoe of Navan for sending me the words when the first version of this book came out.

26. Oh, Limerick is Beautiful 53

'The Mullingar Heifer' is a song about many places: this is about one only – the city on the Shannon which is the second largest in Munster. The air is old and appears in Bunting's collection under the name of 'Rose Connolly'.

It was also used for ballads such as 'Irish Molly, Oh' and 'The Cruise of the Calabar'. The version given here is that of Michael Scanlon, song maker and poet of Limerick, who also wrote 'The Jackets Green'.

27. Cockles and Mussels 54

One of the most famous of Dublin songs, which has received a new lease of life as the adopted 'Anthem' of the crowds at International rugby matches in particular: but indeed at soccer matches too.

VII. THE GIRLS, GOD BLESS 'EM

28. Courtin' in the Kitchen 55

A splendid ballad of comical courtin' and misadventure. It is quite old, having appeared on song sheets by the middle of last century. The tune, known as 'Bobbin' Joan' is even older, having been utilised by John Gay in *Polly*, his successor to *The Beggar's Opera*, early in the eighteenth century.

29. The Bonny Boy 57

One of the sweetest of all Anglo-Irish ballads is to my mind 'The Bonny Boy'. A poignant air, and a simple sadness of words tells us the story of a girl in early widowhood.

30. The Widow of Donaghadee 59

The widow of 'The Bonny Boy' is young and lonesome: we imagine her counterpart of Donaghadee as being older, tougher and altogether more like a woman on a broom.

31. Brian Óg and Molly Bawn 60

Duets in balladry are uncommon enough to be unique and 'Brian Óg and Molly Bawn' is, therefore, worth quoting; apart from the fact that it is a fine bouncy number and a great favourite of mine.

32. The German Clockwinder 62

This rabelisian effort found its way to me through Mrs Brown of Crumlin, Dublin, mother of twenty-two children, one of whom was Christy who, in his short life, overcame the handicap of being spastic with great determination and acquired considerable skill as a painter and author.

33. The Low-Backed Car 63

The best known song of Samuel Lover, who, like Percy French in the generation after him, had a very popular one-man performance for which he wrote his own songs. He died in 1868.

VIII. SONGS FROM TROUBLED TIMES

34. The Man from Mullingar 64

A light-hearted and amusing song from the 'troubled times' of 1916-1922. I got it from the collection which the late Seán Healy left to me when he died in the 1960s.

35. The Boys of Wexford 66

A really stirring song of the rising of 1798 which also has the virtue of being well written. Whether R. D. Joyce (1830-83) wrote it or revised an earlier ballad is not absolutely clear. joyce was a fine virile maker of songs: a poet rather than a ballad maker.

IX. SONGS OF REMEMBRANCE AND HOME

1. Preab San Ól!

Translation: James N. Healy.
Music: Ríobard Bairéad (Richard Barrett)

Those in this game for fortune or fame might spare a thought for how short is life What will it matter midst all this clatter when you're six feet down without child or wife What e-ver your thing Duke, lord or King you'll not take a ha'penny into the ground Forget your troubles they're just life's bubbles and cry 'Let's

fill up with one more round.'

The covetous banker for profits may hanker
But for him the gaining is only a game
It's not that he's needy – he's just being greedy
And the profits he makes are just profits in name.
For the greatest of prophets such method would scoff at
As camels who'd pass through a needle's eye found
So forget all your troubles, they're only life's bubbles
And call for the filling of one more round.

The captain at sea can never feel free
'Tho in harbours all over the world he may hide
From Spain to Gib'ralter or anchored in Malta
Or far Constantinople on the world's other side
For he must set to sea and 'tis then he will see
That death can be master in storm or aground
So forget all your troubles, they're only life's bubbles
And call for the filling of one more round.

The life of a flower is shed by the hour
And brighter the lily the quicker 'twill fade
Yet Solomon's glory 'tho' fabled in story
Could ne'er be so brightly or briefly arrayed
This life with its sins is a puff of the winds
A brief wisp of mist on a hillside around
So forget all your troubles, they're only life's bubbles
And call for the filling of one more round.

1a. Preab San Ól!

by Ríobard Bairéad

Is iomdha slí bhíos ag daoine
A' cruinniú piosaí 's a' déanamh stóir,
's a luíod a smaoiníos ar ghiorra an tsaoil seo,
's go mbéidh siad sínte faoi leac go fóill.
Má's tighearna tíre, diúic nó rí thú,
Ní cuirfíor pínn leat a' dul faoi'n bhfód:
Mar sin 's dá bhrí sin níl beart níos críonna
Ná bheith go síorruí 'cur preab san ól!

An ceannuí craosach níl meón ná slí ar bith
Le ór a dhéanamh nach bhfeichthear dhó
An ráta is daoire ar an earra is saoire,
Is ar luach shé bpíne go gcuirfeadh cróin,
Do réir chaint Chríosta is ní do-dhéanta
An cámhall cíocrach a thabhairt thrid a' gcró;
Mar sin 's dá bhrí sin níl beart níos críonna
Ná bheith go síorruí 'cur preab san ól!

An long thar sáile níl clúid ná ceárd
I nach gcaithfeadh cairde ar feadh an domhain mhóir,
Ó ríocht na Spáinne suas Gibráltar,
Agus ansan áit a mbíonn an Grand Seigniór.
Le gach cárgo líonfadh málaí
Ní choinneódh an bás uaidh uair ná ló;
Mar sin, a cháirde, níl beart níos fearr dhúinn
Ná bheith mar tá sin, 'cur preab san ól!

Is gearr a' saol tá ag a' lili sgiamhach,
Cé gur buí agus gur geal a góil,
Agus Solamh críonna ina chulaí ríoghmhail
Nach bhfuil baol air i n-áille dhó.
Níl sa' tsaol seo ach mar sionán gaoithe,
Gath a sgaoiltear nó slám dho cheó;
Mar sin 's dá bhrí sin níl beart níos críonna
Ná bheith go síorruí 'cur preab san ól!

2. Bottles of Black Porter

Words: Ted Desmond
Air: based on 'The Farmer making Hay'

I was born so small and weak no bottle could I
touch or take Until the nurse the order gave Go
get that child some porter.

And when to Man's estate I grew
My medicine chart no bottles knew,
Nor potions, pills or powders blue
But bottles of plain porter.

Churchill and Dev are two good sports
But when Churchill, very out of sorts,
Asked from Dev, the Irish Ports
Dev told him to stick to porter.

Some fear to swim the river Lee
The Shannon, Boyne or Old Liffey;
But who wouldn't chance the Irish sea
If frothy brine were porter.

Paddy Flaherty on a skite
Travelled pubs by day and night,
But what did he drink when he got tight? –
He called for pints of porter.

11

And now my song has come to an end
My homeward way I soon must wend,
I'm hoping that the Gods will send
Another round of Porter.

Chorus:
Tooriloo, riloo, riloo
Tooriloo, riloo, riloo
Tooriloo, riloo, riloo
O give that child some porter.

3. The Jug of Punch

Words and music: traditional (19th century)

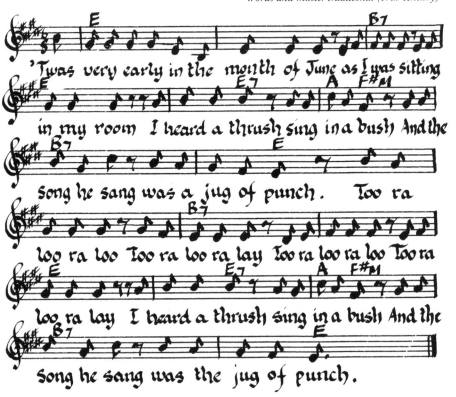

'Twas very early in the month of June as I was sitting in my room I heard a thrush sing in a bush And the song he sang was a jug of punch. Too ra loo ra loo Too ra loo ra lay Too ra loo ra loo Too ra loo ra lay I heard a thrush sing in a bush And the song he sang was the jug of punch.

What more divarsion can a man desire,
Than to be seated by a snug coal fire,
Upon his knee a pretty wench,
And on the table – a jug of punch.
Too ra loo, etc

If I were sick and very bad,
And was not able to go or stand,
I would not think it all amiss,
To pledge my shoes for a jug of punch.
Too ra loo, etc.

The Muses twelve and Apollo famed,
In Castilian pride dhrinks Pernicious sthrames:
But I would not grudge them ten times as much
As long as I had a jug of punch.

The doctor fails, with all his art,
To cure an impression on the heart,
But if life was gone – within an inch –
What would bring it back like a jug o'punch?

But when I am dead and in my grave,
No costly tombstone will I have,
But I'll dig a grave both wide and deep,
With a jug of punch at my head and feet.

Now you jovial topers as you pass by,
If you are thirsty, step in and try,
And with your sweethearts never flinch,
To dip your bills in a jug of punch.
Too ra loo, etc.

13

4. Whiskey in the Jar

Words and music: traditional (late 18th century)

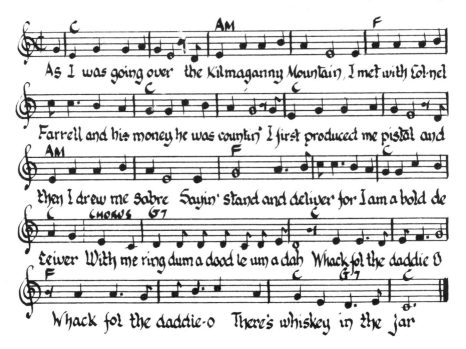

Well, the gold and the silver on the ground it looked so jolly
I gathered it all up, and brought it to my Molly
She promised and she vowed that she would not deceive me
But divil take the women for they never can be easy

I went into her chamber, all for to take a slumber
I dreamt of gold and silver, and for sure it was no wonder.
But Molly took me pistols and filled them up with water
And she sent for Colonel Farrell to be ready for the slaughter.

So next mornin' I awoke at the hour of six or seven
The redcoats stood around me in numbers all uneven
I then produced me pistols, for she stole away me sabre
But I couldn't shoot the water and so I was taken.

Well they threw me into jail without a writ or bounty
For robbin' Colonel Farrell on the Kilmaganny mountain
But they couldn't take me fist, so I knocked down the sentry
And bade no farewell to the Colonel or the gentry.

If I could find my brother who listed in the army
I know that he would aid me in Cork or Killarney
We'd set out for Kilkenny, and no one dare follow
And I'd be much safer with him than with my faithless Molly.

Some take delight in fishin', some take delight in bowlin'
Some like the fields, or the sea that goes a-rollin'
But I take more delight now in the juice of the Barley
Then to courtin' pretty maidens in the mornin' bright and early.

5. The Tipperary Christening

Words and music: traditional

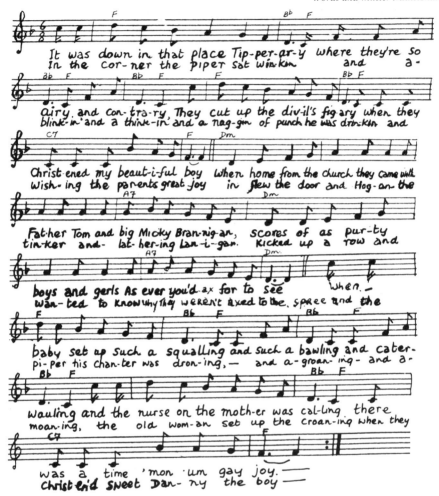

Th' aristocracy came to the party,
There was M'Carty, light and hearty,
Wid Florence Bidalia Fo-garty,
(She says that's the French for her name).
Dionaysius Alphonso Mulrooney,
Oh! so loony and so spoony,
Wid the charming Evangeline Mooney,
Of society she was the crame.
Cora Teresa Maud M'Cann.

Algeron Rourke and Lulu M'Cafferty,
Reginald Marmaduke Maurice Megan,
Clarence Ignatius M'Gurk.
Cornelius Horatio Flaherty's son,
Adelaide Grace and Doctor O'Rafferty,
Eva M'Loughlin, Cora Muldoon, and Brigadier-General Burke.
They were dancing the polka mazurka,
'Twas a worker ne'er a shirker.
The varsovianna la turker,
And the polka row-dow was divine.
They marched and then went in to luncheon,
O, such punchin', and such scrunchin',
They were busy as bees at the munchin',
Wid coffee, tay, whisky, and wine.

There was all sorts of tay, there was Schowchong,
And there was Ningyong, and there was Dingdong,
With Colong, and Toolong, Boolong,
And tay that was made in Japan,
There was sweetmeats imported from Java,
And from Guavre, and from Harve,
In the four-masted ship the Minarva,
That came from beyant Hindostan,
Cowld ice-creams and creams that was hot,
Roman punch froze up in snowballs and sparagrass,
'Patte de foi gras,' whatever that manes,
Made out of goose livers and grease.
Red-headed ducks wid salmon and peas,
Bandy-legg'd frogs and Peruvian ostriches,
Bottle-nosed pickerel, Woodcock and snipe,
And ev'rything else that would plaze,
After dinner, of course, we had spaking,
There was handshaking, there was leave-taking,
In the corner ould mothers matchmaking,
Wid other innocent sins.
And we drank a good health to each other,
Then to each brother, then to each mother,
But the last toast I thought I would smother,
When they hoped that the next would be twins.

6. Lannigan's Ball

Words: George Gavan
Air: Hurry the Jug (traditional)

In the town of Athy one Jeremy Lannigan, Battered away 'til he hadn't a pound His father he died and made him a man again Left him a farm and ten acres of ground He gave a grand party to friends and relations who did not forget him when come to the wall And if you but listen I'll make your eyes glisten at the rows and ructions of Lannigan's Ball

Myself, to be sure, got free invitation
For all the nice boys an' girls that I'd ask,
In less than a minute the friends and relations
Were dancing as merry as bees round a cask.
Miss O'Hara, the nice little milliner,
Tipp'd me a wink to give her a call,
And soon we arrived with Timothy Galligan,
Just in time for Lannigan's ball.

They were doing all kinds of nonsensical polkas
All round the room in a neat whirligig;
But Julia and me soon banished nonsense
And tipp'd them a twist of a real Irish jig.
Och Mavrone, 'twas she that was glad o' me,
And danced till you'd think the ould ceiling would fall;
For I spent a whole fortnight at Burke's Academy,
Larnin' a step for Lannigan's ball.

The boys were all merry, the girls were all hearty,
Dancing away in couples and groups,
Till an accident happened young Terence McCarthy,
He put his right leg on Miss Flaherty's hoops,
The creature she fainted – roared milia murder,
Called for her friends and gathered them all,
Ned Carmody swore that he'd go no further,
But he'd have satisfaction at Lannigan's ball.

In the midst of the row Miss Kerrigan fainted,
Her cheeks all the while being as red as a rose,
Some of the ladies declared she was painted,
She took a small drop too much, I suppose.
Her sweetheart, Ned Morgan, so powerful and able,
When he saw his fair colleen stretched by the wall,
He tore the leg from under the table,
And smashed all the *chaney at Lannigan's ball.

Oh, boys, there was a ruction,
Myself got a kick from big Phelim M'Cue,
But soon I replied to this kind introduction,
And kicked up a terrible Phillabooloo;
Ould Casey the piper was near being strangled,
They squeezed up his pipes, bellows, chanters, and all;
The girls in their ribbons were all entangled,
And that put an end to Lannigan's ball.

*china

7. De Night before Larry was Stretched

Words: attributed to William Maher ('Hurlfoot Bill')

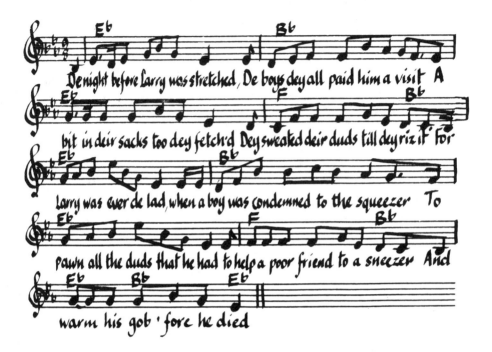

De night before Larry was stretched, De boys dey all paid him a visit A bit in deir sacks too dey fetch'd Dey sweated deir duds till dey riz it For Larry was ever de lad, when a boy was condemned to the squeezer To pawn all the duds that he had to help a poor friend to a sneezer And warm his gob 'fore he died

De boys came crowding in fast,
Dey drew all deir stools round about him,
Six glims on his trap-case were placed, –
He could not be well waked without 'em
When one of us asked could he die
Without having duly repented?
Says Larry, 'Dat's all in my eye;
And first by the clergy invented,
To get a fat bit for themselves.'

'I'm sorry, dear Larry,' says I
'To see you in this situation;
And blister my limbs if I lie,
But I'd lieve it had been my own station.'
'It's all over wid me,' says he,
'The neckcloth I'll be forced to put on,
And by this time tomorrow you'll see
Your poor Larry quite dead as de mutton,'
Because, why, his courage was good.

20

'And I'll be cut up like a pie,
And my nob from my body be parted.'
'You're in the wrong box, den,' says I,
'For blast me if dey're so hard-hearted:
A chalk on de back of your neck
Is all that Jack Ketch dares to give you;
Den mind not such trifles a feck,
For why should the likes of dem grieve you?
And now, boys, come tip us the deck.'

De cards being called for, dey played,
Till Larry found one of dem cheated;
A dart at his napper he made –
De lad being easily heated:
'So ye cheats me bekase I'm in grief!
O, is dat, be de hokey, de reason?
Soon I'll give you to know, you damn'd theif
Dat you're crackin' your jokes out of season
And scuttle your knob with me fist!'

Then comes the clergy with book,
He spoke him so nate and so civil;
Larry tipped him a bloody sour look,
And pitched his big wig to the devil;
Then sighing, he threw back his head
To get a sweet drop of the bottle,
He sighing most heavily said,
'O, the hemp will be soon round my throttle,
And sqeeze my poor windpipe to death.'

'Dough sure it's the best way to die, –
De devil a better a-livin'!
For sure, when the gallows is high
Your journey is shorter to heaven!
But what harasses Larry the most,
And makes his poor soul melancholy,
Is to tink of the time when his ghost
Will come in a sheet to sweet Molly;
'O sure it will kill her alive!'

His last words so meltingly spoke
Our grief it found vent in a shower
As for my part, I thought my heart broke
To see him cut down like a flower.
On his travels I watched him next day;
De throttler, I thought I could kill him;
But never a word did he say,
Nor changed till he come to 'King William,'
Den his colour began to grow white!

When he came to de numbing chit,
He was tucked up so neat and so pretty,
The rumbler shoved off from his feet,
And he died wid his face to de city
And kicked, too – but dat was all pride,
For soon you might see 'twas all over;
And when dat de noose was untied,
At dark why we waked him in clover
And sent him to take a ground sweat.

NOTES:
'Sweated deir duds' – pawned their clothes.
'De Squeezer; De Hemp; De neck-cloth' – the rope of Jack Ketch, the hangman.
'a sneezer' – presumably a pinch of snuff.
'warm his gob' – warm his mouth (with a drop of whiskey).
'the rumbler' – in those days the 'drop' had not been invented. The victim stood on a cart which
was driven away from under him. Hanging on the rope, he strangled slowly.

8. Finnegan's Wake

Words: mid 19th century – traditional
Tune: traditional

22

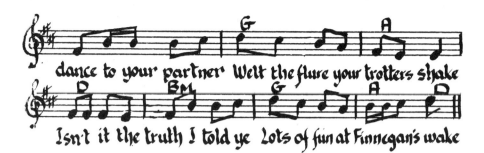

dance to your partner Welt the flure your trotters shake

Isn't it the truth I told ye Lots of fun at Finnegan's wake

One morning Tim was rather full;
His head felt heavy, which made him shake,
He fell from the ladder, and broke his skull,
So they carried him home a corpse to wake.
They rolled him up in a nice clean sheet,
And laid him out upon the bed,
With fourteen candles around his feet,
And a gallon of porter at his head.
Chorus:

His friends assembled at his wake;
Missus Finnigan called for the lunch.
First they laid in tea and cake;
Then pipes and tobacky, and whisky-punch,
Miss Biddy O'Brien began to cry;
'Such a decent corpse did ever you see?
Arrah! Tim avoureen, an' why did ye die?'
'Och, none of your gab,' sez Billy Magee.
Chorus:

Then Peggy O'Connor took up the job,
'Arrah! Biddy,' says she, 'ye'er wrong, I'm shure,'
But Biddy then gave her a belt on the gob,
And left her sprawling on the flure.
Each side in war did soon engage,
'Twas woman to woman and man to man,
Shillelah-law was all the rage –
An' a row an' ruction soon began.
Chorus:

Mickey Mulvaney raised his head,
When a gallon of whiskey flew at him.
It missed him – and hopping on the bed,
The liquor scattered over Tim!
Bedad he revives! see how he rises!
An' Timothy, jumping from the bed,
Cried, while he lathered around like blazes:
'In the name of the divil! d'ye think I'm dead.'
Chorus:

9. Tá na Lá ('Tis the Day)

Original Irish – traditional
New translation – James N. Healy

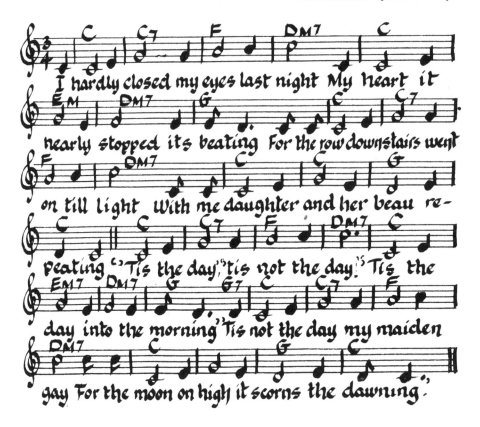

I hardly closed my eyes last night My heart it nearly stopped its beating For the row downstairs went on till light With me daughter and her beau repeating "'Tis the day", "'tis not the day." 'Tis the day into the morning 'Tis not the day my maiden gay For the moon on high it scorns the dawning.

Chorus:
> ''Tis the day! ''Tis not the day!'
> ''Tis the day and into the morning.'
> ''Tis not the day, my maiden gay!
> For the moon on high it scorns the dawning.'

A Boozer:
> 'Get up, O man of the house, get up.
> Get up and put on your breeches.
> The party's swinging, give us a sup.
> We'll reward you with plenty of riches.'

Landlord:
> 'I won't get up,' sez the man of the house,
> 'I won't put on me breeches.
> Never the drop will I give to carouse,
> Not for all King Solomon's riches.'

Boozer:	'Me socks are in pop in the pawnbrokers shop And me shoes have to pay me call; Me fences tell down, cows o'er them hop And I've ne'er a wifeen at all!'
Another Boozer:	'The barrel is empty, of that I'm sound. Bar dirty old dregs we'd be scorning. So here's a pound to stand a round And let us drink on 'till the morning!

9a. Tá na Lá ('Tis the Day)

Traditional

(Fear an tairne)
'Ó! chodlas féin i dtigh aréir,
Is tuirseach tréith do bhí mo chuisle:
Comhrá béil bhí 'cu go léir,
M'inghean féin 's a boc ar buile.'

(Inghean agus Pótairí)
'Tá 'n-a lá' 'Níl 'n-a lá!'
'Tá 'n-a lá agus 'n-a mhaidin!'
'Níl 'na-lá, dheara, a ghrá,
Ach solus árd atá sa' ghealaigh!'

(Pótaire)
'Éir' id shuí, 'fhir a' tighe,
Cuir do bhríste 'mut go tapaidh,
Coinnigh suas cuideachta shuairc
Do chroí mhaith mhór go dtíocfaidh an mhaidean!'

(Fear an táine)
'N'éireód im shuí,' ar fear a' tighe,
''S ní chuirfead bríste 'mum ná hata,
Blas ná braon dem chuid-se dighe
A raghaidh na gcroí go dtiocfaidh an mhaidean!'

(Pótaire)
'Tá mo stocaí i dtigh an óil,
Tá mo bhróga i dtigh an leanna,
Tá mo bha a' dul thar téorainn,
Is níl bean óg a raghadh dá gcasa!'

(Pótaire eile)
'Tá an barraille thar a cheann,
Is ní fheicim ann ach dríodar dearga
Tá mo ghiní ar an mbórd,
Is bíom ag ól go dtiocfaidh an mhaidean!'

10. Pléaráca na Ruarcach (O'Rourke's Feast)

Original Irish Words: Aodh Mac Gabhráin (Hugh Mac Gowran)
This translation: James N. Healy. Music by Carolan

The feast of O'Rourke is remembered by many Who came or is gone or who never was there Seven score pigs, sides of beef and fresh mutton were killed for the gluttons and nothing left spare Gallons of whiskey and casks full of vino From dawn of the morning such rat-i-tee-tat Your pipe it was broken my pocket was opened Your breeches were stolen Well who burned me hat? Sure I lost me old cloak and me shirt and me garters My

handkerchief too but we'll let that one pass Let us
sing, let us dance, come along with the snuff box and
come on sweet Annie and fill up me glass

The sons of O'Rourke were all solid in slumber
When they first heard the rattle and bang of the band
They leaped out of bed without even an Ave
And fondled the women on every hand
God knows how the floor held up under their trampling
Or don't split apart with the gurgling of ale
Good health and good luck to you Loughlin O'Finnegan
And Marcella's dancing did never yet fail.
Here's to your mother, I toast you, God save you
Fill up the bowl, and let's drink to the dregs
Stretch out the bed for us, cover us over
When the power goes out of our tottering legs.

O High King of Heaven! but you should have seen them
When their bellies were filled with the maddening drink
Then the knives were drawn out with a flashing and stabbing
And the long staves were whacking as quick as a wink
'You beggar! my father build churches at Sligo,
And at Galway and Boyle and at Carrick as well.'
The guests and the hosts started belting each other
Arguing, roaring and wishing to hell
'The Earl of Kildare and the chief of Moynalty
Gave me aid and protection – just ask of the lass'
O take down the sounder and beat the alarm;
A fist in the guts and a boot up the ass!

'Who raised the alarm' bellowed one of the clergy
Jumping out of his seat with a threatening roar
And it wasn't a prayer book he took to assail them
But a stout lump of wood from the back of the door
But the fighters had gone beyond blessing or reason
So under the table they threw the bold friar
And the Guardian and brothers who thought to assist him
Were dumped on their bellies on top of the fire!

'While we were in Rome to receive Holy Orders
With blessings of Popes and of Bishops galore
'Twas little we thought we'd be frying like potatoes
On top of the fire beyond in Sheemore!'

10a. Pléaráca na Ruarcach

Words by Aodh Mac Gabhráin.
Music by Carolan

Pléaráca na Ruarcach i gcuimhne gach uile dhuine
Dá dtiocfadh, dá dtáinic, 's dá maireann go fóill:
Seacht bhfichid muc, mart agus caora
Dhá gcasgairt don ghasraí gach aon ló.
Céad páil usige bheatha 's na meadra dhá líona,
Ag éirghe ar maidin is againn bhí an spóirt
Briseadh do phiopa-sa, sladadh mo phóca-sa,
Goideadh do bhríste sa, loisgeadh mo chlóca sa,
Chaill mé mo bhairéad, m'fhallaing is m'fhiléad,
Ó d'imigh na gairéad ar seacht mbeannacht leó!
Cuir spraic ar a' gcláirsigh, seinn suas a' pléaráca,
An bucsa sin, 'Áine, 'gus greadóg le n-ól!'

Lucht leanamhna na Ruarcach a'craitha a gcleití,
Tráth chuala siad tormán no troimpléasg an cheóil;
D'éirigh gach aon aca gan coisreaca 'n-a leabaidh,
Is a bhean leis ar strachailt in gach aon chórn.
Nár láidir an seasamh don talamh bhí fútha,
Gan réaba le sodar agus glug ins gach bróig!
Saol agus sláinte dhuit, 'Mh'leachhlainn Uí Fhionnagáin,'
Dar mo láimh is maith a dhamhsuíos tú, 'Mhársail Ní Ghriodagáin!
Here's to you, 'mháthair, I pledge you, God save you!
Beir ar a' sgála so, sgag é in do sgóig.
Craith fúinn an tsráideóg, sin tharuinn an bhán-phluid,
Tugthar ar sáith dhúinn de lionn-choirm chóir!

A Árd-Rí no gcarad, cébi 'tchifeadh an ghasraí
Ar líona a gcraiciní nó ar lasa san ól!
Cnáimh righe bacaird ar fad in gach sgín aca,
A' gearra 's a' cosgairt go mór, mór, mór;
A slisneacha darach ar lasa a'gabháil fríd a chéile,
A' buala, a' greada, a' losga 's a dódh.
A bhodaigh, 'sé m'athair-se chuir Mainistir na Búille suas,
Sligeach is Gaillimh is Caraidh Dhroma Rúisgthe fós.
Iarla Chill' Dara agus Biadhtach Mhui n-Ealta,
Siad d'oil agus d'altruim mé, fiosraigh so de Mhór.
Tóid suas a' t'ádhmad agus buail an t-alárm air,
Preab ionsa táirr agus cic ionsa tóin!

'Cé thóig a' t-alárm so?' ar aon den Eaglais,
Ag éirghe 'n-a sheasamh 's a' bagairt go mór;
Ní h-é spairgeas uisge coisreactha ghlac sé sa gcíora
Ach bata maith darach, bog-lán dóirn!
Tráth shíl se na caithmhílidh a chasgairt 's a chíora,
Do fágadh an sagart 'n-a mheall chasta fan mbórd.
D'éirigh na bráithre a' tárrtháil na bruíne,
Is fágadh an t-Athair Gáirdain ar a thárr 'n-áirde sa ngríosaí!
'Tráth bhínn-se ag an bPápa ar stuidéar na ngrásta,
'S a' glaca na ngrádhamh tháill ins a' Róimh,
'S an Seven Wise Masters bhí agad ar do tháirr,
Is tú a' rósta na bprátai láimh leis a' tSidh Mhór!

29

11. The Bard of Armagh

Words and music: traditional (19th century)

Oh list to the lay of a poor Irish harper and scorn not the
strings in his old withered hands But remember those
fingers could once move more sharper to waken the
echoes of his dear native land

It was long before the Shamrock, our green isle's loved emblem
Was crushed in its beauty, neath the Saxon lion's paw.
It was called by the colleens of the village and valley,
Bold Phelim Brady, the Bard of Armagh.

How I long to muse on the days of my boyhood,
Though four score and three years have flitted since then,
Still it gives sweet reflections, as every young joy should,
That merry-hearted boys make the best of old men.

At a pattern or fair I could twist my shillela,
Or trip through a jig with my brogues bound with straw
Whilst all the pretty maidens around me assembled,
Loved Bold Phelim Brady, the Bard of Armagh.

Although I have traveled this wide world over,
Yet Erin's my home and a parent to me,
Then oh! let the ground that my old bones shall cover
Be cut from the soil that is trod by the free.

And when Sergeant Death in his cold arms shall embrace me,
To lull me to sleep with sweet Erin go bragh,
By the side of my Kathleen, my young wife, O place me,
Then forget Phelim Brady, the Bard of Armagh.

12. The Shilling a Night

Words: Eoghan Roe Ward
Air: The Ould Orange Flute

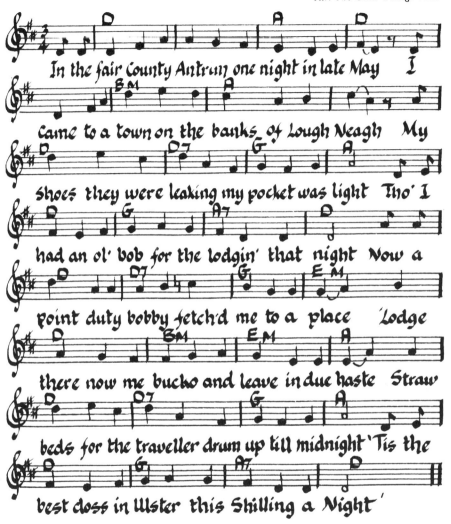

In the fair County Antrim one night in late May I
came to a town on the banks of Lough Neagh My
shoes they were leaking my pocket was light Tho' I
had an ol' bob for the lodgin' that night Now a
point duty bobby fetch'd me to a place 'Lodge
there now me bucko and leave in due haste Straw
beds for the traveller drum up till midnight 'Tis the
best doss in Ulster this Shilling a Night'

Faith the Widow Maloney had no fear of God,
She looked at my whiskers, and grabbed for my bob,
She got my twelve coppers and yelled with delight,
''Tis the rent of a farm, a Shilling a Night.'

Troth the Widow Maloney, I had her to know,
If the workhouse was goin', 'tis there I would go,
Shure a bath and a clean shirt and me sore feet put right,
There was divil the likes in her Shilling a Night.

'Ough, my foxy Owen Roe, ye dacent young man,
This house is me own, go to blazes ye can,
There's no better in Antrim, ye can search till daylight,
An' me company is grand in the Shilling a Night.'

'Faith Widow Maloney, 'tis known fine well,
You keep the worst scratch from Loop Head to Clonmel,
You've Rangoons and Highlanders, who come by moonlight
And torture poor souls in the Shilling a Night.'

To the bed I crept hungry, the traveller's fate,
And lay down nearly twelve stone, but arose only eight,
For her 'Panzers' attacked me with bite after bite,
And drank all me blood in the Shilling a Night.

With the grey dawn of morning, I arose nearly wild,
My skin was as black, as a nigger was boiled,
With a curse on me lips, from oul' Antrim took flight,
For I had met me match in the Shilling a Night.

13. John Twomey's drinking song

Free Translation by James N. Healy
Air: Óldan Seán Ó Tuama

To every one a full measure Not drinking, then what is your
pleasure You're short did you say Can't afford it today What
harm you can pay at your leisure So
fill up your glass with the brandy Too much, yirra think 'tis a
Shandy I've money enough to pay for the stuff and to
sing an oul ballad I'm handy

I love an oul' tap of the toe
And there's sport in the brandy – ho! ho!
Now, now, do not spill it
Good gerl Maggy, fill it.
And here's to the Bards that we know.

And like those old songsters begone
Let's have divilment, drinking and song
Could one of ye try
A Ballad, bi-em-bye
To help a gay evening along?

13a. Ól-Dán Seán Ó Tuama

Words: Seán Ó Tuama (John Twomey of Croom)
Seán Bhean críon an Brantáin (The Nagging Old Woman)

Ar duine mé Dhíolas liún lá
'S chuirios mo bhiudhin chuin ran-gáis
   Muna m-beidheadh amháin duine
   Am chuideachta dhíolfadh
Is mise bheidheadh síos leis an am-tráith

Taosgaidh bhúr n-dóithin de'n m-brandán
Bhúr n-deocha ná tomhasaidh le ban lámh
   Tá 'gamsa sgilling
   Le leigion san bh-fíon n-glan
'S as fearr ioná 'n bhuidhin bhídeas ag drantán

Do b'ait liomsa ceólta 'na dh-tiompán
Do bh'ait liomsa spórt agus brandán;
   Do bh'ait liomsa an gloine
   Ag murrainn dá líonadh
'S cuideachta saoite gan mheabhrán.

Ag aithris éolais na sean-dámh
Carbhas, ól, agus abhrán;
   Fuirion an ghliocais,
   Ag imirt na laoithe,
Súd mar do ghrídhin-si gach íon-tlás.

14. An Bunnán Buíde – The Yellow Bittern

Original by Cathal Buíde Mac Giolla Gunna
Translation by Thomas MacDonagh

34

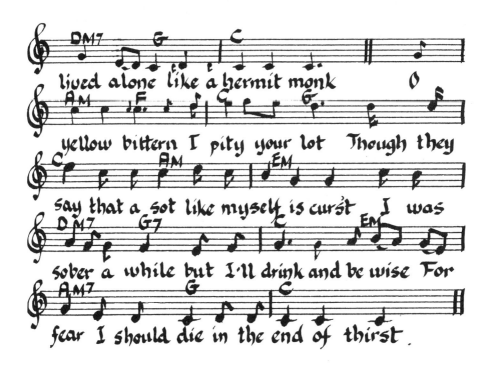

It's not for the common birds that I'd mourn,
The blackbird, the corncrake or the crane,
But for the bittern that's shy and apart
And drinks in the marsh from the lone bog-drain.
Oh! if I had known you were near your death,
While my breath held out I'd have run to you,
Till a splash from the lake of the Son of the Bird
Your soul would have stirred and waked anew.

My darling told me to drink no more
Or my life would be o'er in a little short while;
But I told her 'tis drink gives me health and strength,
And will lengthen my road by many a mile.
You see how the bird of the long smooth neck
Could get his death from the thirst at last -
Come, son of my soul, and drink your cup,
For you'll get no sup when your life is past.

14a. An Bunnán Buíde

by Cathal Buíde MacGiolla Gunna

A bhunnáin bhuí, 'sé mo léan do luí
'Gus do chnámha sínte ar leacach lom.
'S ní dteárn tú díth ná dolaí sa' tír
Is nár bhfearr leat fíon ná uisge poll.
Ó! bhitheá a' síor-ól na dighe,
'Gus deir siad go mbím ar an nós sin seal,
'S níl braon dá bhfuíod nach leigfead síos,
Ar eagla go bhfuínn féin bás don tart.

Ní h-aid bhur n-éanlaith 'tá mé 'éagcaoin
Nár chuir spéis araimh sa' digh,
Ach an bunnán léana bhíodh leis féin
Ag ól go réidh ar na curraigh amuigh.
Dá gcuirtheá sgéala fá mo dhéin
Go raibh tú i bpéin, bhéinn in mo ruith
Nó go mbainnin béim as Loch Mhic an Éin
A fhliucfadh do bhéal is do chorp istigh.

'Se dúirt mo stór liom leigean don ól,
'S nach mbéinn-se beo ach seal beag gearr.
Agus dúirt mé léithi gur chan sí bréag,
Gur bhfuide dom shaol an braon dighe 'fháil.
Nach bhfeic tusa éan an phíobáin réidh,
Go ndeacha sé dh'éag don tart ar ball?
'S a dhaoine chléibh, Ó! fliuchaigí bhur mbéal,
Ní bhfuí sibh braon i ndéidh bhur mbáis!

36

15. The Oul' Triangle

Words and music by Brendan Behan (from his play 'The Quare Fella')

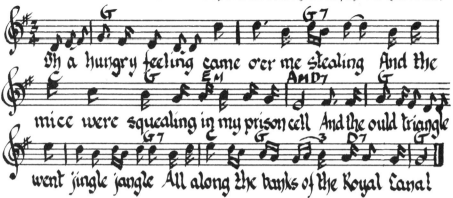

To begin the morning the warder bawling
'Get out of bed and clean up your cell'
And that old triangle
Went jingle jangle
Along the Banks of the Royal Canal.

On a fine spring evening the lag lay dreaming
The seagulls wheeling high above the wall
And that old triangle
Went jingle jangle
Along the Banks of the Royal Canal.

The screw was peeping and the lag was sleeping
While he lay weeping for his girl Sal
And that old triangle
Went jingle jangle
Along the Banks of the Royal Canal.

The wind was rising and the day declining
As I lay pining in my prison cell
And that old triangle
Went jingle jangle
Along the Banks of the Royal Canal.

The day was dying and the wind was sighing
As I lay crying in my prison cell
And that old triangle
Went jingle jangle
Along the Banks of the Royal Canal.

In the female prison there are seventy women
I wish it was with them that I did dwell
And that old triangle
Could go jingle jangle
Along the Banks of Royal Canal.

16. The Bould Tadhy Quill

Words: traditional
Air: 'Do b'Fhearr Leigean dóibh'

Ye maids of Duhallow who're anxious for courtin', a word of advice I will give unto ye Proceed to Banteer to the athletic sportin' and hand in ye'er names to the club committee But do not comm--ence any sketch of your progress till a carriage you see comin' over the hill And down thro' the valleys and hills of Kil--corney, With that Muskerry sportsman, the Bould Tadhy Quill. For ramblin', for rovin', for football or sportin', for emptin' a bowl sure as fast as you'd fill In all your days scovin' you'd find none so jovial, As the Muskerry sportsman the Bould Tadhy Quill.

Tadhy was famous in many other places;
At the athletic meeting held out in Cloghroe
He won the long jump without throwing off his braces
Goin' fifty-four feet every sweep he would throw.
At the puttin' of the weight there was a Dublin man foremost,
But Tadhy outreached and exceeded him still
And around the whole field rang the wild ringin' chorus
Here's luck to our Hero, the bound Tadhy Quill

At the great hurlin' match between Cork and Tipperary
'Twas played in the Park by the Banks of the Lee
Our own darlin' boys were afraid of being beaten
So they sent for bould Tadhy to Ballinagree
He hurled the ball left and right in their faces
And show'd those Tipp'rary boys learnin' and skill
If they came in his way, shure he surely would brain' em
And the papers were full of the praise of Tade Quill.

In the year '91 before Parnell was taken,
Tade was outrageously breakin' the peace;
He got a light sentence for causin' commotion
And six months hard labour for batin' police.
But in spite of coercion he's still agitatin' –
Ev'ry drop of his life's blood he's willin' to spill
To gain for ould Ireland complete liberation
'Till then there's no rest for me Bould Tadhy Quill.

At the Cork Exhibition there was a fair lady,
Whose fortune exceeded a million or more;
But a bad constitution had ruined her completely
And medical treatment had failed o'er and o'er.
'Oh, Mama,' said she 'I know what'll cure me
And all me diseases most certainly kill.
Give over your doctors and medical treatment
I'd rather one shake outa bould Tadhy Quill.'

39

17. The Wren Boy's Song

Traditional

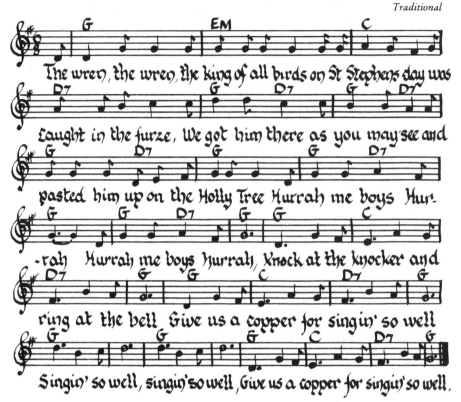

The wren, the wren, the king of all birds on St Stephens day was caught in the furze, We got him there as you may see and pasted him up on the Holly Tree Hurrah me boys Hurrah Hurrah me boys hurrah, Knock at the knocker and ring at the bell Give us a copper for singin' so well Singin' so well, singin' so well, Give us a copper for singin' so well.

I have a little box under me ar-um
Two or three pence would do it no har-um;
Up with the kettle and down with the pot,
Give us our answer and let us be off. *Chorus:*

On Christmas day I turned the spit
I burned me finger – I feel it yet!
Between me finger and me thumb
There lies a blister as big as a plum. *Chorus:*

God bless the mis'tus (mistress) of this house –
A golden chain around her neck –
If she's sick or if she's sore,
The Lord have mercy on her soul. *Chorus:*

Mrs. . . a worthy man
And to her house we bring the wran,
Although he's little his family's great
Come out Mrs. . . and give us a treat. *Chorus:*

18. The Night the Goat Broke Loose on Grand Parade

Words: unknown
Air: 'Brian of and Molly Bawn' (part)

Paddy McGinty bought a house and lived in Sunday's Well Sit-u

ated on the Northside of the Lee He lived all alone in his cosy little

home So he bought a goat to keep him company Now says

Paddy to the goat for you I'll buy a coat and a visit to Cork

City we will pay But the goat kicked up a mountain when he

saw the Berwick Fountain Oh the night the goat broke

loose on Grand Parade Oh the night the goat broke

loose on Grand Parade All the people in Cork City got afraid

For the shout went through the country That the Glen had won the

County on the night the goat broke loose on Grand Parade

Mary Ellen Warner stood at Woodford Bourne's corner
Said she 'I'll catch the train to Dublin or I'll die.'
But the goat came up behind her and he gave her such a winder
That she hadn't time to bid her friends good-bye.
Mary Ann Fitzgibbon had her drawers all torn to ribbons
A-running to the Munster Arcade
And it was a sad bereavement
When he tumbled her on the pavement
On the night the goat broke loose on Grand Parade.

Chorus:
On the night the goat broke loose on the Parade
Poor Mary Ann Fitzgibbon got afraid
She went tearin' down the Coal Quay
'Shure 'twas worse than any Polka
The Night the Goat broke loose on the Parade.

Now the people up in Barrack Street when they heard the dreadful news
Swore out in vengeance what they'd do
They lined the streets in batches, all armed with saws and hatchets
But when the goat appeared they all withdrew.
Oh, the goat came round the corner and he thundering like a cannon
Followed by the Cork Fire Brigade
When he came up to the South Gate Pier, he tumbled into the weir
And was never seen again on Grand Parade.

Final Chorus:
Oh the night the goat broke loose on the Parade
All the ladies and the gents they were dismayed
And Mary Ann Fitzgibbon's
Clothes were torn in ribbons
On the night the Goat broke loose on the Parade.

19. Stickin' out a Mile from Blarney

Words and Music: Traditional

Now Shandon Steeple stands up straight
And ould Fair Lane runs undernate
If you ask for fish they'll give you mate
Stickin' out a mile from Blarney. *Chorus:*

Now what did Peter say to Paul
When he hopped from the window on to the wall?
'How's yer ould wan'? 'She's game ball'
Stickin' out a mile from Blarney. *Chorus:*

43

20. Dear Old City by the Lee

Words and music: origin not known

Dear Cork City by the Lee what I would not give to
be roaming over your sunny hills and dells listening
to the merry chimes as we did in days gone by when our
hearts they were full of liberty Montenotte and St Lukes they
might attract your looks: Fair Lane, Barrack Street and Evergreen
From the Courthouse to the College they have different sorts of
knowledge And yet the half of Cork you have not seen

And also so they say
There is the famed Coal Quay
There's a restaurant there that's famous for pig's feet
Where you get a feather bed,
And a fine feed of pig's head
But don't forget to pay before you leave.

44

And so we turn our feet
Up to the North Main Street
As we walk up Shandon Street to Sweet Blackpool
They have medals by the score
Won eight 'counties' in a row
And here's to the boys of Sweet Blackpool.

And now before we finish
We'll have a pint of Beamish
Murphy and Guinness is good too.
But I'll never forget the oil
I had with Connie Doyle
The Night we won the Junior County Cup!

21. The Pretty Girls of Cork

Words: John Fitzgerald
Air: 'Nora Creina'

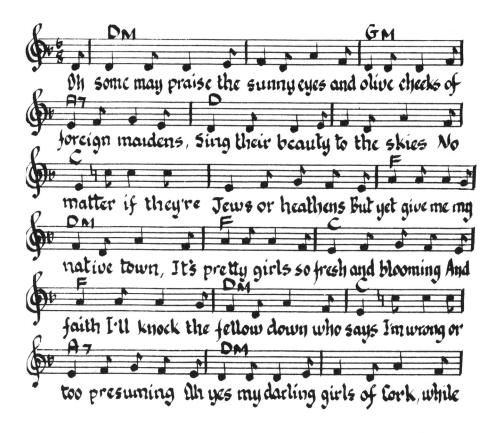

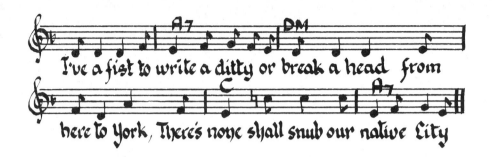

I've a fist to write a ditty or break a head from
here to York, There's none shall snub our native City

Talk not to me of Spanish dames,
Or hint about the fair Circassian,
And all their odd Jaw-breaking names,
Or, faith, you'll put me a passion.
But see our ladies as they walk,
And look upon their pretty faces,
And listen to their charming talk –
Reminding you of nymphs and graces.
Ah, yes, the darlings, one and all,
Are just like beds of perfumed flowers;
And if you have a heart at all,
You'll lose it in a brace of hours.

In sweet Blackpool, famed for 'de Groves',
(Though, troth, I never yet could find them),
You'll meet with handsome girls in droves,
That leave all other girls behind 'em.
And sure the land of fat drisheens –
May nothing ever take them from us –
Has lasses that are fit for queens –
The bouncing girls of Ballythomas.
Aye, there you're sure to take your choice,
And don't let trifles love diminish,
If there's a roughness in their voice,
They're gems that only want the finish.

There are beauties living on the Marsh.
(Where you might vainly look for rushes),
Who're not too cold, nor proud, nor harsh,
Who dance like fays, and sing like thrushes.
And if they wear the largest 'hoops',
'Tis not for want of shape and form –
To see them meet in pretty groups,
The cockles of your heart would warm.
Indeed, 'Twould break your heart with sighs,
To see such girls and not caress them –
To look upon such lips and eyes,
And not do something to possess them.

46

If you are blest with any taste,
You'll show a stranger, while he tarries,
Those darlings with the slender waist –
The roaring belles of 'sweet Sinbarry's'.
And if he strolls through Evergreen.
Among potatoes, leeks and cabbages,
And say that fairer girls he's seen –
Dear knows, he's only just a savage.
They talk a deal about the girls
They meet upon a foreign shore,
But, faith, 'tis treating swine to pearls
To tell them they're as good next door.

Then, hey for Cork, its streets and quays,
Its 'Shandon Bells' and meadows green,
Its girls and their coaxing ways,
Its boys that sip the sweet potheen,
Its ever-sparkling River Lee,
And world-famed 'Ould Blarney Stone',
Its poets (not forgetting me),
To make its varied beauties known.
Aye, faith, my darling girls of Cork,
While I've a fist to write a ditty,
Or break a head from here to York,
There's none shall snub our native City.

22. The Boys from County Cork

You've read in hist'ry's pages of the heroes of great fame The deeds they done, the battles won and how they made their name But the boys who gave a hist'ry to the Orange White and Green Are the boys who died in Dublin Town in Nineteen and Sixteen

Chorus:
There were some of the boys from Kerry, some of the boys from Clare,
From Dublin, Wicklow, Donegal, and boys from old Kildare.
There were boys from the land beyond the seas from Boston and New York
But the boys who bate the Black and Tans were the boys from County Cork.

Cork gave us MacSwiney, a hero he did die,
Wicklow gave us Michael Dwyer in the days so long gone by,
Dublin gave us Padraic Pearse, MacBride and Cathal Brugha
And America De Valera for to lead ould Ireland through. *Chorus:*

We seem to be divided, I really don't know why,
We've a glorious list of martyrs, who for Ireland did die;
Now why not get together and join in unity
The North, the South, the East and West will set ould Ireland free. *Chorus:*

23. The First Cork Brigade

Words: attributed to Miceál Barrett
Air: 'John Brown's Body' (The Battle Hymn of the Republic)

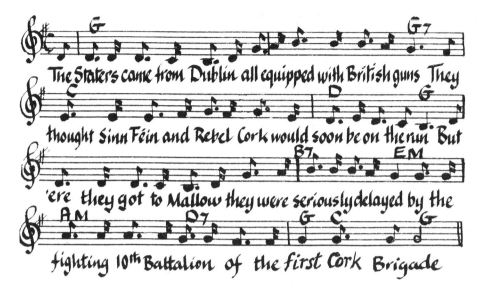

The Staters came from Dublin all equipped with British guns They thought Sinn Féin and Rebel Cork would soon be on the run' But 'ere they got to Mallow they were seriously delayed by the fighting 10th Battalion of the first Cork Brigade

Chorus:
Glory, Glory to old Ireland
Glory, Glory to our Sireland
Glory, Glory to the men who fought and fell
'No Surrender' is the war cry of the First Cork Brigade.

When John Bull sent his gunmen to shoot McCurtain down
He thought Sinn Féin was dead and gone in this old Rebel town
He thought he had us to the wall but we were not afraid
'No Surrender' is the war cry of the First Cork Brigade.

We have no Shiney Gaiters and no Sam Brown belts to show
But we're able to defend ourselves no matter where we go
We're out for a Republic and to Hell with the Free State
'No Surrender' is the war cry of the First Cork Brigade.

They bombed us in the alleys, and they bombed us in the Glen
They bombed us out at Dillons Cross, and we bombed 'em back again
They bombed us down on Pana, and on the Grand Parade
And we gave 'em 'who began it' in the First Cork Brigade.

49

24. Old Skibbereen

Words and music: traditional

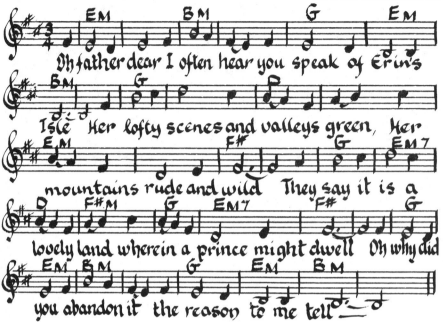

Oh father dear I often hear you speak of Erin's Isle Her lofty scenes and valleys green, Her mountains rude and wild They say it is a lovely land wherein a prince might dwell Oh why did you abandon it the reason to me tell

Oh, son! I loved my native land with energy and pride,
Till a blight came o'er my crops – my sheep, my cattle died;
My rent and taxes were too high, I could not them redeem,
And that's the cruel reason that I left old Skibbereen.

Oh, well do I remember the bleak December day,
The landlord and the sheriff came to drive us all away;
They set my roof on fire with their cursed English spleen,
And that's another reason that I left old Skibbereen.

Your mother, too, God rest her soul, fell on the snowy ground,
She fainted in her anguish, seeing the desolation round,
She never rose, but passed away from life to mortal dream,
And found a quiet grave, ay boy, in dear old Skibbereen.

And you were only two years old and feeble was your frame,
I could not leave you with my friends – you bore your father's name –
I wrapt you in my cotamore at the dead of night unseen,
I heaved a sigh and bade good-bye, to dear old Skibbereen.

Oh, Father dear, the day may come when in answer to the call
Each Irishman, with feeling stern, will rally one and all:
I'll be the man to lead the van beneath the flag of green,
When loud and high we'll raise the cry – 'Remember Skibbereen'.

25. The Mullingar Heifer

Words: unknown
Air: Toor-al-i-ay

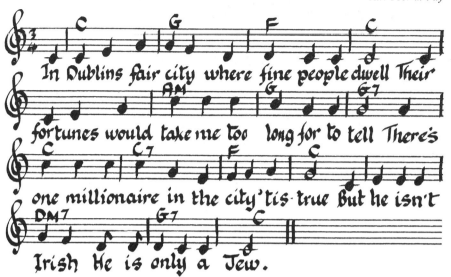

In Dublins fair city where fine people dwell Their
fortunes would take me too long for to tell There's
one millionaire in the city 'tis true But he isn't
Irish He is only a Jew.

The people of Limerick have got a fine name
Their hams and their bacons are well known to fame
Their sausages too are the finest of meat
While the people of Dublin eat only pig's feet.

Old Maguire of Clonmel was that fond of his bed
His poor wife he nearly drove off of her head
At last for the villian she did prove a match
For she gave him twelve duck eggs and told him to hatch.

The Kilkenny lads are fine rovin' blades
And make a good match for the Kilkenny maids
And when they get married they all wear silk hats
To rear up the kittens of the Kilkenny cats.

A Belfast girl said 'a blonde I'd like to be'
So she bought a bottle at a swell pharmacy,
Something exploded her peroxide
She thought she was dead but she only was dyed.

When a Galway girl got married in days long dead
She got for her fortune a fine feather bed,
When a girl now gets married they think it enough
To give her a lipstick and a new powder puff.

There was an elopement down in Mullingar
But sad to relate the pair didn't get far
'Oh fly,' said he, 'Darling and see how it feels.'
But the Mullingar heifer was beef to the heels.

A barber in Trim used get gay with the girls
Who came to his parlour to shingle their curls
His wife caught him giving a permanent wave
Now the poor fellow lies in a permanent grave.

A Cork lad who stammered was once getting wed
And he practised beforehand the words to be said
'Will you take this woman,' the parson did press
And he had to say 'no' because he couldn't say 'yes. . .es'.

26. Oh, Limerick is Beautiful

Words: Michael Scanlon
Air: 'Irish Molly, Oh'

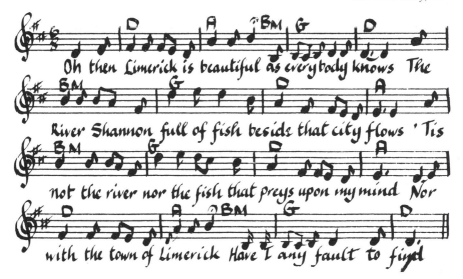

Oh then Limerick is beautiful as everybody knows The
River Shannon full of fish beside that city flows 'Tis
not the river nor the fish that preys upon my mind Nor
with the town of Limerick Have I any fault to find

'Tis not for Limerick that I sigh –
Though I love her in my soul –
Though times will change and friends will die,
And man will not control;
No, not for friends long passed away,
Or days for ever flown,
But that the maiden I adore
Is sad in Garryowen.

Oh! she I love is beautiful,
And world-wide is her fame;
She swells down by the rushing tide,
And Eire is her name;
And dearer than my very life
Her glances are to me,
The light that guides my weary soul
Across life's stormy sea.

I loved her in my boyhood,
And now in manhood's noon
The vision of my life is still
To dry thy tears, aroon
I'd sing unto the tomb, or dance
Beneath the gallows tree,
To see her on the hills once more
Proud, passionate and free.

27. Cockles and Mussels

Words and music: traditional

In Dublin's fair city, where girls are so pretty, I first set my eyes on sweet Molly Malone As she wheel'd her wheel barrow through streets broad and narrow, Crying cockles and mussels alive alive oh Alive, alive oh Alive, alive oh Crying cockles and mussels Alive, alive oh.

She was a fishmonger,
But sure it was no wonder,
For so were her father and mother before.
And they both wheeled their barrow
Through the streets wide and narrow,
Crying 'Cockles and mussels, alive, alive, oh.'

She died of a fever,
And none could relieve her,
And that was the end of sweet Molly Malone.
But her ghost wheels her barrow,
Through the streets broad and narrow,
Crying 'Cockles and mussels, alive, alive, oh.'

28. Courtin' in the Kitchen

Words: unknown
Air: Bobin' Joan

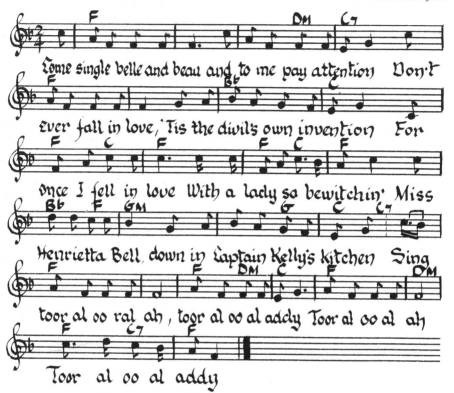

Come single belle and beau and to me pay attention Don't ever fall in love, 'Tis the divil's own invention For once I fell in love With a lady so bewitchin' Miss Henrietta Bell, down in Captain Kelly's kitchen Sing toor al oo ral ah, toor al oo al addy Toor al oo al ah

Toor al oo al addy

At the age of seventeen
I was 'prenticed to a grocer
Not far from Stephens Green
Where Miss Bell she used to go, sir.
Her manners were so fine
She set me heart a-twitchin'
When she axed me out to tea
Down in Captain Kelly's kitchen.

Sunday bein' the day
We were to have the flare-up
I dressed meself quite gay
And frizzed and oiled me hair up.
The Captain had no wife
And he'd gone off a-fishin'
So we kicked up high-life,
Below stairs in the kitchen

Just as the clock struck six
We sat down to the table.
She handed tea and cakes –
I ate what I was able.
I had cakes with Punch and tay
'Till me side had got a stitch in
And the time passed quick away
With our courtin' in the kitchen.

With me arms around her waist
I kissed – she hinted marriage –
When to the door in haste
Came Captain Kelly's carriage:
Her looks tol' me full well
– and they were not bewitchin' –
That she wished I'd get to hell,
Or somewhere from the kitchen.

She flew up off my knee,
Full five feet up or higher,
And over head and heels
Threw me slap into the fire.
My new Repealer's coat
That I bought from Mr Mitchel
With a thirty-shilling note
Went to blazes in the kitchen.

I grieved to see me duds
All besmeared with smoke and ashes,
When a tub of dirty suds
Right in me face she dashes.
And as I lay on the floor
The water she kept pitchin',
'Till a footman broke the door
And came chargin' in the kitchen.

When the Captain came downstairs,
'Tho he seen me situation,
Despite of all me prayers
I was marched off to the station.
For me they'd take no bail,
'Tho to get home I was itchin',
And I had to tell the tale
Of how I came into the kitchen.

I said she did invite me
But she gave a flat denial;
For assault she did indict me,
And I was sent for trial.
She swore I robbed the house
In spite of all her schreechin',
And I got six months hard
For me courtin' in the kitchen.

29. The Bonny Boy

Words and Music – traditional (19th century)

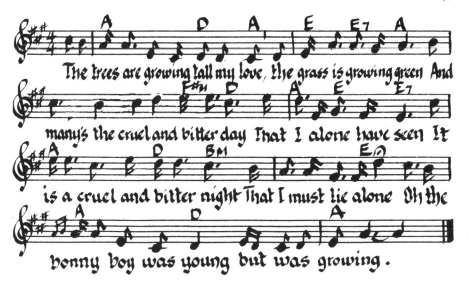

The trees are growing tall my love, the grass is growing green And many's the cruel and bitter day That I alone have seen It is a cruel and bitter night That I must lie alone Oh the bonny boy was young but was growing.

Oh Father, my father, indeed
You did me wrong
For to go and get me married
To one who is so young
He being only sixteen years
And I being twenty-one
He's a bonny, boy, but young –
And still growing.

My daughter, my daughter
I did not do you wrong
For to go and get you married
To one who is so young
He will be a match for you
When I am dead and gone
He's a bonny boy, he's young –
But he's growing

Oh Father, my father,
I'll tell you what I'll do
I'll send my love to college
For another year or two
And all around his college cap
I'll tie a ribbon blue
Just to let the ladies know
That he's married.

At evening when strolling
Down by the college wall
You'd see the young collegiates
A-playing at the ball
You'd see him in amongst them there
The fairest of them all
He's my bonny boy, he's young,
But he's growing.

At the early age of sixteen years
He was a married man,
At seventeen the father of
A darling baby son
At eighteen years – t'was over –
O'er his grave the grass grew strong,
Cruel death put an end
To his growing.

I will buy my love a shroud
Of the ornamental brown
And whilst they are making it
My tears they will run down
That once I had a true love
But now he is gone
And I'll mind his bonny boy –
While he's growing.

30. The Widow of Donaghadee

Words: traditional
Air: 'Toor-al-i-ay'

There was an old widow in Donaghadee And in her back garden a row of plum trees But the widows big dog was a tied to its roots and the town ladies they wore a nip of its roots. Too ra loo Too ra lee Oh it's six miles from Bangor to Donaghadee.

So she bought a wee horse and she went thro' the town
Selling apples and oranges all the way round
And she'd crack her old whip and sit twisting her thumbs
'Till the town folk were shy of her garden and plums
Too-ra-loo etc.

But one day a ship sailed in close to the quay,
It had run from a voyage far away on the sea,
The poor half-starved sailors they made for the shore,
And dropped like the devil on the old widow's door.
Too-ra-loo etc.

She gave them some soup and she gave them some tea,
She dry baked the oaten as quick as could be,
A quart of fine whiskey as they picked up the crumbs,
Then from her back garden she brought in her plums.
Too-ra-loo etc.

They ate all those plums till their tummies were sore,
In anger the skipper made for the back door.
He cursed and he raved and he tore up the root
And a hundred bright sovr'igns he picked up as loot.
Too-ra-loo etc.

And now all you listeners take warning from me,
I sailed round the world and on many a sea,
Many plums I have sampled as ripe as could be,
But the best plums of all came from Donaghadee.
Too-ra-loo etc.

31. Brian Óg and Molly Bawn

Words: traditional
Music: early 19th century

Oh come listen to my story Molly Bawn For I'm bound for death of glory, Molly Bawn For I've listed in the army where no more eyes can harm me, Faith they'd kill me though they charm me, Molly Bawn.

Molly: Wisha Brian, you've been drinking now, you rogue
I can tell it by your winking, Brian Óg,
But you'd ne'er be such a villian as to take the Saxon Shillin'
And to do their dirty killin', Brian Óg.

And shure what will all the boys say, Brian Óg,
That you've turned a red-coat h'athen, Brian Óg,
Go list so, if it please you, ach ya villian, do not tease me
Sure you'd drive a cailín crazy, Brian Óg.

Brian: 'Twas yourself that drove me to it, Molly Bawn,
When you read my death you'll rue it, Molly Bawn
When I die mid' foemen wrestlin' where the balls like hail are whistlin'
Aye, and bloody bayonets bristlin', Molly Bawn.

And the last words I'll be speakin', Molly Bawn,
When me soul its leave is takin', Molly Bawn,
'An Grádh mo Croidhe mo Storín your old Sweetheart Brian Ógín
For you his blood is pourin', Molly Bawn

Molly: Shure I done it all to prove you, Brian Óg,
But I hate – Oh no, I love you, Brian Óg,
But keep up your heart, a Cara, for I'll buy you out tomorrow
'Tho I die of shame and sorrow Brian Óg.

And to think that you should doubt me, Brian Óg
And meself so wild about you, Brian Óg,
Would you let that thief Phil Dornan come and wed me in the mornin'
Faith you might have given me warnin' Brian Óg.

Brian: Oh I'm strong and hale and hearty, Molly Bawn
Sure I'm one like Bonaparty, Molly Bawn
And the divil a list I listed, for the sergeant tried and missed it
And your mind, now, you've confessed it, Molly Bawn.

Molly: Sure I'm kilt right out with schamin', Brian Óg,
It's me self that thinks it shamin', Brian Óg,
Since you didn't take the shillin' just to save your life I'm willin'
To get wed. *(They kiss)* Behave you villian Brian Óg.

32. The German Clockwinder

Words: *unknown*
Air: *variant of 'Toor-al-i-ay'*

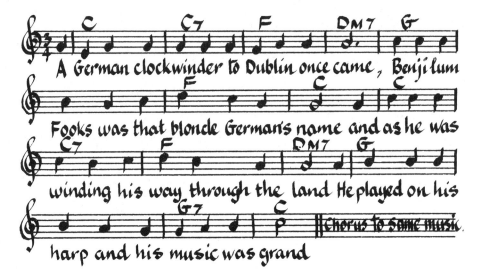

A German clockwinder to Dublin once came, Benji lum
Fooks was that blonde German's name and as he was
winding his way through the land He played on his
harp and his music was grand

Chorus:
With your tool-a-lumma,
Tool-a-lumma, tool-lil-iaye.

Oh, there was a young lady from Grosvenor Square
Who said that her clock was in need of repair,
In walks the blonde German and to her delight
In less then five minutes he had her put right. *Chorus:*

Now as they were seated down on the floor
There came this very big knock on the door,
In walked her husband and great was his shock
To find the blonde German had wound his wife's clock. *Chorus:*

The husband says he 'Now look here, Mary Jane,
Don't let that blonde German in here again.
He wound up your clock and left mine on the shelf,
If you oul' clock needs winding I'll wind it meself!' *Chorus:*

33. The Low Backed Car

Words and music: Samuel Lover

When first I saw sweet Peggy, 'twas on a market day A low-back'd car she drove and sat upon a truss of hay But when the hay was blooming grass and deck'd with flowers of spring No flow'r was there that could compare with the blooming girl I sing As she sat in her low back'd car The man at the turnpike bar, Never asked for his toll, but just rubb'd his old poll and look'd after the low-back'd car.

In battle's wild commotion,
The proud and mighty Mars,
With hostile scythes, demands his tithes,
Of death – in warlike cars;
While Peggy, peaceful goddess,
Has darts in her bright eyes,
That knock men down, in the market town,
As right and left they fly –
While she sits in her low-backed car,
Than battle more dangerous far –
For the doctor's art
Cannot cure the heart
That is hit from that low-backed car.

Sweet Peggy, round her car, sir,
Has strings of ducks and geese
But the scores of hearts she slaughters
By far out-number these;
While she among her poultry sits,
Just like a turtle dove,
Well worth the cage, I do engage
Of the blooming god of love
While she sits in her low-backed car,
The lovers come near and far
And envy the chicken
That Peggy is pickin',
As she sits in the low-backed car.

O, I'd rather own that car, sir,
With Peggy by my side
Than a coach-and-four and gold galore*,
And a lady for my bride;
For the lady would sit forninst** me,
On a cushion made with taste,
While Peggy would sit beside me
With my arm round her waist –
While we drove in the low-backed car,
To be married by Father Maher,
Oh, my heart would beat high
At her glance and her sigh –
Though it beat in a low-backed car.

* in plenty   ** before

34. The Man from Mullingar

Words and music: origin unknown

You may talk and write and boast about your Fenians and your clans and
how the boys of county Cork beat up the Black and Tans and
view a little codger who came out without a scar His

name was Paddy Mulligan the man from Mullingar And the
peeler's chased him out of Connemara For
beating up the valiant scion O'Hara And he came to Ballymote He
stole the parson's goat and sold him to the Bishop down in
Ardagh Seven hundred peelers' cousins henchmen The
King sent out an order for to lynch him When
Patrick came to Dublin Park, he sold his motor car And
gave it to the I.R.A Brigade in Mullingar.

On Easter Monday when the boys did hear the bugle's sound
Paideen raised the flag of war down in his native town.
First he went to make his peace with dear old Father Maher,
Then went out and blew the barracks up, and wrecked half Mullingar. *Chorus:*

When Ireland takes her place among the nations of the world,
And her flag of orange, white and green to the four winds is unfurled,
When you read the roll of honour you will find mark'd with a star
Patrick Sarsfield Mulligan, the man from Mullingar! *Chorus:*

35. The Boys of Wexford

Air: traditional
Words: attributed to Robert D. Joyce

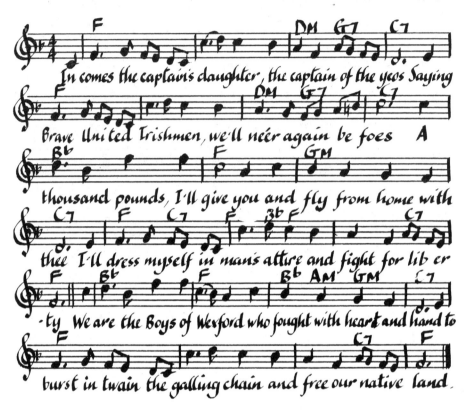

In comes the captain's daughter, the captain of the yeos Saying Brave United Irishmen, we'll néer again be foes A thousand pounds, I'll give you and fly from home with thee I'll dress myself in man's attire and fight for lib er -ty We are the Boys of Wexford who fought with heart and hand to burst in twain the galling chain and free our native land.

And when we left our cabins, boys,
We left with right goodwill,
To see our friends and neighbours
That were at Vinegar Hill!
A young man from our ranks,
A cannon he let go;
He slapt it into Lord Mountjoy –
A tyrant he laid low!
We were the boys of Wexford,
Who fought with heart and hand,
To burst in twain the galling chain,
And free our native land!

66

We bravely fought and conquered
At Ross, and Wexford town;
And, if we failed to keep them,
'Twas drink that brought us down.
We had no drink beside us
On Tubberneering's day,
Depending on the long bright pike,
And well it worked its way!
We are the boys of Wexford,
Who fought with heart and hand
To burst in twain the galling chain,
And free our native land!

They came into the country
Our blood to waste and spill;
But let them weep for Wexford,
And think of Oulart Hill!
'Twas drink that still betrayed us –
Of them we had no fear;
For every man could do his part
Like Forth and Shelmalier!
We are the boys of Wexford,
Who fought with heart and hand
To burst in twain the galling chain,
And free our native land!

My curse upon all drinking!
It made our hearts full sore;
For bravery won each battle,
But drink lost evermore;
And if, for want of leaders,
We lost at Vinegar Hill,
We're ready for another fight,
And love our country still!
We are the boys of Wexford,
Who fought with heart and hand
To burst in twain the galling chain,
And free our native land!

36. The Croppy Boy

Words and music: traditional (19th century)

I twas very early in the spring The birds did whistle and sweetly sing

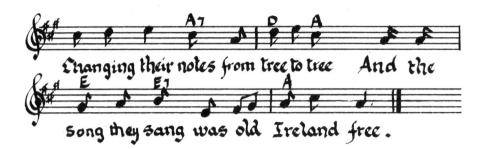

Changing their notes from tree to tree And the
song they sang was old Ireland free.

It was early, early in the night,
The yeoman cavalry gave me a fright;
The yeoman cavalry was my downfall,
And taken was I by Lord Cornwall.

'Twas in the guard-house where I was laid,
And in a parlour where I was tried;
My sentence passed and my courage low
When to Dungannon I was forced to go.

As I was passing by my father's door,
My brother William stood at the door;
My aged father stood at the door,
And my tender mother her hair she tore.

As I was walking up Wexford Street
My own first cousin I chanced to meet;
My own first cousin that did me betray,
And for one bare guinea swore my life away.

My sister Mary heard the express,
She ran upstairs in her mourning-dress –
Five hundred guineas I will lay down,
To see my brother through Wexford Town.

As I was walking up Wexford Hill,
Who could blame me to cry my fill?
I looked behind and I looked before,
But my tender mother I shall ne'er see more.

As I was mounted on the platform high,
My aged father was standing by;
My aged father did me deny,
And the name he gave me was the Croppy Boy.

It was in Dungannon this young man died,
And in Dungannon his body lies;
All you good Christians that do pass by
Just drop a tear for the Croppy Boy.

37. The Rising of the Moon

Words: John K. Casey ('Leo')
Air: The Wearing of the Green

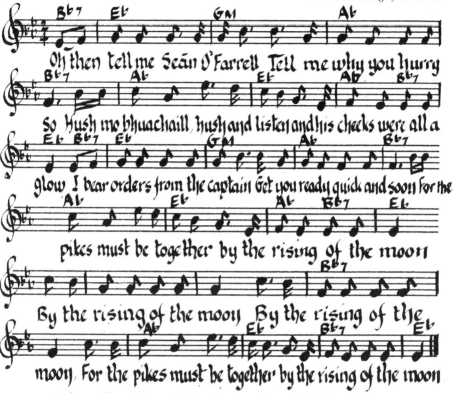

'O then, tell me, Shawn O'Farrell, where the gath'rin' is to be?'
'In the old spot by the river, right well known to you and me;
One word more – for signal token, whistle up the marchin' tune,
With your pike upon your shoulder, by the risin' of the Moon.'

Out from many a mud-wall cabin eyes were watching through that night;
Many a manly heart was throbbing for the blessed warning light.
Murmurs passed along the valleys, like the banshee's lonely croon,
And a thousand blades were flashing at the risin' of the Moon.

There, beside the singing river, that dark mass of men was seen –
Far above the shining weapons hung their own beloved Green,
'Death to every foe and traitor! Forward! strike the marchin' tune,
And hurrah, my boys, for freedom! 'tis the risin' of the Moon.'

Well they fought for poor old Ireland, and full bitter was their fate;
(O what glorious pride and sorrow fills the name of 'Ninety-Eight!)
Yet, thank God, e'en still are beating hearts in manhood's burning noon,
Who would follow in their footsteps at the risin' of the Moon!

38. Whack fol-the-Diddle

Words and music: Peadar Kearney

When we were savage, fierce and wild,
Whack fol the diddle lol the di do day.
She came as a mother to her child,
Whack fol the diddle lol the di do day.
Gently raised us from the slime,
Kept our hands from hellish crime,
And sent us to heaven in her own good time,
Whack fol the diddle lol the di do day. *Chorus:*

Our fathers oft' were naughty boys,
Whack fol the diddle lol the di do day
Pikes and guns are dangerous toys,
Whack fol the diddle lol the di do day.
From Baile Atha Buidhe to Pieters Hill
They made poor England weep her fill,
But old Britannia loves us still,
Whack fol the diddle lol the di do day. *Chorus:*

Oh Irishmen forget the past,
Whack fol the diddle lol the di do day
And think of the day that is coming fast,
Whack fol the diddle lol the di do day
When we shall all be civilised
Neat and clean and well advised,
Oh won't Mother England be surprised!
Whack fol the diddle lol the di do day. *Chorus:*

39. Brennan on the Moor

Words and music: traditional (early 19th century)

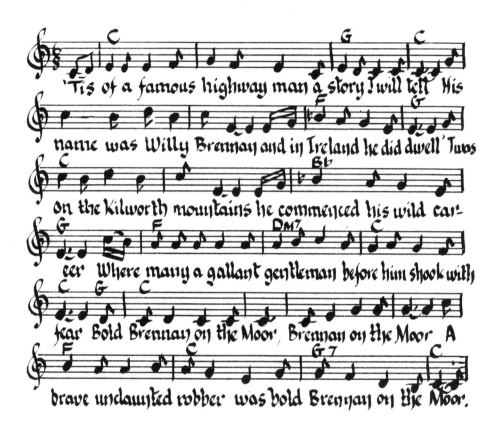

'Tis of a famous highway man a story I will tell His name was Willy Brennan and in Ireland he did dwell 'Twas on the Kilworth mountains he commenced his wild career Where many a gallant gentleman before him shook with fear Bold Brennan on the Moor, Brennan on the Moor A brave undaunted robber was bold Brennan on the Moor.

A brace of loaded pistols he carried night and day;
He never robbed a poor man upon the king's highway;
But what he'd taken from the rich, like Turpin and Black Bess,
He always did divide it with the widow in distress.

One night he robbed a packman, of the name of Pedlar Bawn;
They travelled together till the day began to dawn;
The pedlar seeing his money gone, likewise his watch and chain,
He at once encountered Brennan, and robbed him back again.

Now Brennan seeing the pedlar as good a man as he
He say, 'My worthy hero, will you come along with me?'
The pedlar, being stout-hearted, he threw his pack away,
And he proved a loyal comrade until his dying day.

One day on the highway, as Willy he sat down,
He met the Mayor of Cashel, a mile outside the town,
The Mayor, he knew his features – 'I think, young man,' said he,
'Your name is Willy Brennan – you must come along with me.'

As Brennan's wife had gone to town provisions for to buy
When she saw her Willy, she began to weep and cry,
He says, 'Give me that tenpenny' as soon as Willy spoke
She handed him a blunderbuss from underneath her cloak.

Then with his loaded blunderbuss, the truth I will unfold,
He made the Mayor to tremble, and robbed him of all his gold.
One hundred pounds was offered, for his apprehension there,
And he with his horse and saddle, to the mountain did repair.

Then Brennan being an outlaw upon the mountain high,
The cavalry and infantry to take him they did try;
He laughed at them with scorn, until at length, it's said,
By a false-hearted woman he basely was betrayed.

Then Brennan and his companion, when they were betrayed,
They with the mounted cavalry a noble battle made:
He lost his foremost finger, which was shot off by a ball,
So Brennan and his comrade they were taken after all.

In the County Tipperary, at a place they call Clonmore,
Willy Brennan and his comrade that day did suffer sore:
He lay amongst the fern, which was thick upon the field,
And nine wounds he did receive before that he did yield.

So they were taken prisoners, in irons they were bound
And conveyed to Clonmel Jail, strong walls did them surround,
They were tried and found guilty – the Judge made his reply:
'For robbing on the king's highway you're both condemned to die.'

When Brennan heard his sentence, he made this reply: –
'I own that I did rob the rich, and did the poor supply;
In all the deeds that I have done I took no life away:
The Lord have mercy on my soul against the judgement-day.

'Farewell unto my wife, and to my children three
Likewise my aged father – he may shed tears for me:
And to my loving mother – who tore her grey locks and cried,
Saying, "I wish, Willy Brennan, in your cradle you had died." '

40. The Moon Behind the Hill

Words: William Kenealy

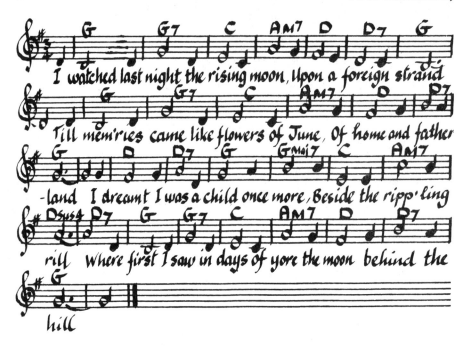

I watched last night the rising moon, Upon a foreign strand
Till mem'ries came like flowers of June, Of home and father-land
I dreamt I was a child once more, Beside the ripp'ling rill
Where first I saw in days of yore the moon behind the hill

It brought me back the visions grand
That purpled boyhood dreams;
Its youthful loves, its happy land,
As bright as morning's beams.
It brought me back my own sweet Nore,
The castle and the mill,
Until my eyes could see no more
The moon behind the hill.

It brought me back a mother's love,
Until, in accents wild,
I prayed her from her home above
To guard her lonely child;
It brought me one across the wave,
To live in memory still –
It brought me back by Kathleen's grave,
The moon behind the hill.

41. Mush Mush

Words and music: traditional (mid-early 19th century)

Oh 'twas there I learned readin' and writin' at Bill Brackets where I went to school. And 'twas there I learned howlin' and fightin' from my schoolmaster Mister O' Toole. Him and me, we had many a scrimmage and the divil a copy I wrote. There was ne'er a garsún in the village dared tread on the tail o' me. Mush mush mush tu-rul-i ady. Singin' mush mush mush, tu-ral i ay. There was ne'er a garsún in the village dared tread on the tail o' me coat.

Oh 'twas there that I learnt all my courtin',
Many lessons I took in the art;
'Till Cupid, the blackguard, in sportin'
An arrow drove straight 'thro me heart.
Molly Connor, she lived right forninst me
And tender lines to her I wrote,
If you dare say one hard word agin her,
I'll tread on the tail of your. . . *Chorus:*

But a blackguard called Mickey Maloney
Came and stole her affections away,
He had money and I hadn't any,
So I sent him a challenge next day.
That evening we met be the woodbine,
The Shannon we crossed in a boat,
And I leathered him with my shillelah,
For he trod on the tail of my. . . *Chorus:*

Oh, my fame went abroad thro' the nation,
And folks came a-flocking to see,
And they cried out without hesitation
'You're a fightin' man, Billy McGee.'
I cleaned out the Finnegan faction
And I licked all the Murphy's afloat,
If you're in for a row or a ruction,
Just tread on the tail o' me. . . *Chorus:*

There are several good reasons for drinkin'
And another one enters me head
If a fella can't drink while he's living
How the hell can he drink when he's dead. *Chorus:*

42. I'll tell me Ma

Words amd air: traditional 19th century (children's game)

I'll tell me ma when I go home, the boys won't leave the girls alone. They toss'd my hair and stole my comb But that's all right till I go home She is hand some, She is pretty, She is the belle of Belfast city. She is courtin' one, two, three, Please won't you tell me whoisshe

(a girl was nominated by the leader – circle resumed, dance)

> The rain may rain, the wind blows high
> The snow comes falling from the sky
> . . . . says she'll die
> If she won't get the lad with the roving eye
> She is fair, she is pretty
> She is the pride of all Cork City
> She is loved by one, two, three
> Break up and tell us who 'twill be

(circle broke up – nominated girl, gave the name of a boy. This name was then used in the following verse)

> . . . . says he'll have her
> All the boys are fighting for her
> Let them all say what they will
> But. . . . has her still.

(above continued until all girls in the circle had been 'dealt with' and then the first part was sung again). No doubt other lines and verses were added in various parts of the country, and the completed version now used for public performance runs like this:

> I'll tell my ma when I go home,
> The boys won't leave the girls alone
> They pulled my hair, they stole my comb,

And that's all right till I go home.
She is handsome, she is pretty;
She is the belle of Belfast city,
She is courtin' one, two, three.
Please won't you tell me who is she.

Albert Mooney says he loves her,
All the boys are fighting for her,
They rap at the door and they ring at the bell,
Saying 'O my true love are you well.'
Out she comes as white as snow,
Rings on her fingers, bells on her toes,
Old Johnny Murray says she'll die,
If she doesn't get the fellow with the roving eye.

Let the wind and the rain and the hail blow high
And the snow come travelling from the sky,
She's as nice as apple-pie,
And she'll get her own lad bye and bye.
When she gets a lad of her own,
She won't tell her ma when she gets home,
Let them all come as they will,
But 'tis Albert Mooney she loves still.

43. The Parting Glass

Words : unknown (late 18th century)
Air: Sweet Cootehill Town

O all the money e'er I had I spent it in good company and
all the harm I've ever done Alas it was to none but me And
all I've done for want of wit To mem'ry now I can't recall So
fill to me the parting glass Good night and joy be with you all

If I had money enough to spend
And leisure time to sit awhile,
There is a fair maid in this town
That sorely has my heart beguiled.
Her rosy cheeks and ruby lips
I own she has my heart in thrall
Then fill to me the parting glass
Goodnight and joy be with you all!

Oh, all the comrades e'er I had
They're sorry for my going away:
And all the sweethearts I e'er had
They'd wish me one more day to stay,
But since it falls unto my lot
That I should rise and you should not.
I gently rise and softly call—
Goodnight and joy be with you all.

OSSIAN PUBLICATIONS

Publishers and Distributors of Irish & General Music

Ossian Publications produce a large range of Irish Music
for traditional & classical instruments as well as
collections of tunes, songs, instruction books and items on
the history of Irish Music.

For our complete list of Books, Sheetmusic,
Cassettes, CDs etc, send us an (international)
postal reply coupon and your name and address.

Ossian Publications Ltd.
P.O. Box 84, Cork, Ireland
E-Mail: ossian@iol.ie

O S S I A N